INTRODUCTION

Work can be fulfilling or frustrating. It can be an instrument of God or a tool of the devil. Work has created great technological breakthroughs—electricity, indoor plumbing, trains, planes, automobiles, artwork, literature, architecture, vaccines, modern surgical procedures, computers, and the Internet. Work has also created detrimental products for society—pornography, violent weapons of mass destruction, and Ponzi schemes.

Wherever work resides on the continuum of our satisfaction scale, it is a necessary component of Christ's plan for our life. We are instructed by the Word of God to not eat unless we work. In the wisdom of the Lord's grand design for humankind, He knows we need work to keep us busy with what is beneficial for our fellow citizens and to keep us from trouble. Work is God's way to display His glory and to give good to His children.

"For even when we were with you, we gave you this rule: 'The one who is unwilling to work shall not eat'" (2 Thessalonians 3:10).

You were created by God and for God to find pride in your work. You know you can be proud of your work when you work as unto to the Lord. A job well done invites the commendation of Christ, "Well done, my good and faithful servant." You bring honor and glory to the ultimate owner of your business and work as you execute excellent work. You steward well your gifts and skills when your labor reflects the Lord's expectations.

I struggle with knowing the sweet spot of my service. Can my passion for a particular type of work align with my calling from Christ? Yes, indeed, but I find myself unable to get to the place of total fulfillment in my current career. But being content and remaining faithful where I am is God's game plan. I do my best and trust Him with the rest so I can rest in Him. He will open doors when I am ready to walk through to His next assignment.

"See, the Lord has chosen Bezalel ... and he has filled him with the Spirit of God, with wisdom, with understanding, with knowledge and with all kinds of skills—to make artistic designs for work" (Exodus 35:30-32).

So as you face work challenges, keep your focus on Christ and His character. God does not waste pain but uses it to grow you into the image of His Son Jesus. Furthermore, leverage your workplace influence for the Lord. Humbly stand on the platform of your outstanding work creations and point to your Creator. He is the author and finisher of all you do well for Him. Faithful is He who has called you, for He will get it done for His glory!

"Make it your ambition to lead a quiet life: You should mind your own business and work" (1 Thessalonians 4:11).

OTHER BOOKS BY BOYD BAILEY

Seeking Daily the Heart of God, Volume I – a 365-day Devotional
Seeking Daily the Heart of God, Volume II – a 365-day Devotional
Infusion – a 90-day Devotional
Seeking God in the Psalms – a 90-day Devotional
Seeking God in the Proverbs – a 90-day Devotional
Wisdom for Graduates – a 30-day Devotional
Wisdom for Mothers – a 30-day Devotional
Wisdom for Fathers – a 30-day Devotional
Wisdom for Marriage – a 30-day Devotional

JOIN OUR ONLINE COMMUNITY

SIGN UP for your free "Wisdom Hunters...Right Thinking" daily
devotional e-mail at **wisdomhunters.com**
"LIKE" us on Facebook at **facebook.com/wisdomhunters**
FOLLOW us on Twitter at **twitter.com/wisdomhunters**
SUBSCRIBE to us on YouTube at
youtube.com/wisdomhuntersvids
DOWNLOAD the free Wisdom Hunters App for
iPhone and iPad on iTunes

TABLE OF CONTENTS

1

Giant Opportunities

The Lord said to Moses, "Send some men to explore the land of Canaan, which I am giving to the Israelites...." Then Caleb silenced the people before Moses and said, "We should go up and take possession of the land, for we can certainly do it." But the men who had gone up with him said, "We can't attack those people; they are stronger than we are."
Numbers 13:1-2, 30-31

As we face life, we can be overwhelmed by its giant obstacles or be inspired by its giant opportunities. Challenges and uncertainty tend to corrode our confidence. It is in the face of the unknown that we can move forward by faith or backward in disbelief. What giant obstacles are you facing? How can your obstacles be converted into opportunities? Obstacles are stepping-stones for obedient feet to follow.

Therefore, stay focused with aggressive patience, and you will eventually see some obstacles dissolve and others transformed into treasures. Maybe a financial giant is looming large as an intimidating obstacle. If so, stay true to your integrity by not selectively suspending your core values for much needed results. Instead, remain faithful to wise stewardship and honesty, and the right results will follow at the right time. Trust God to use scary giants for His glory.

God orchestrates giant opportunities for His greater good. He told Moses that He was giving His children the Promised Land; all they had to do was show up and receive His gift. Giant opportunities do require faith, planning, perseverance, and hard work, as the reward of obedience and trust in the Lord is enough. So how are you facing the giants in your life—as obstacles or opportunities?

Leaders look and pray for opportunities and then explore them with energy and enthusiasm. Your relentless leadership inspires your family, friends, and work associates to remain faithful and not freak out. Therefore, take the land of opportunity the Lord has given you. Difficult days and economic challenges are greater opportunities for God to get the glory. So be aggressive, increase your efforts, pound heaven in prayer, and by faith receive what your Savior Jesus has already given you. Go after the giant opportunities with gusto and by grace.

The Bible says, "I can do all things through Him who strengthens me" (Philippians 4:13 NASB).

What giant obstacle can I trust God to turn into an opportunity?

Related Readings: Joshua 14:6-8; Isaiah 41:10-16; Romans 8:31-37; Hebrews 11:33

2

God-Sized Goals

Jesus replied, "What is impossible with men is possible with God."
Luke 18:27

God-sized goals are meant to challenge our thinking and further our faith. These "big ideas" inspired by the Holy Spirit are crafted by our Creator to spur us on to good works and transformational living. God-sized goals make us uncomfortable at times. They are not guaranteed to happen, but they position us to pray more and believe in God better.

It is through prayerful planning and implementation that gigantic goals move from mere possibility to a surer probability. Huge objectives are a hedge against mediocrity and a prod toward perfection. God-sized goals are given to govern your thinking and determine your time so you are intentional and focused on His big picture. Otherwise, you can drift around without a rudder of reality, destined to disappointment.

Best of all, God-sized goals get you to God. It is prayer and planning with significant progress that move you from the realm of possibility to the place of probability. In most cases, it is one man or woman's passion and focus that prove catalytic to the creation and execution of the goals. The leader looks failure in the eye and extinguishes it by faith, wisdom, and hard work, which are all wrapped around a skilled and unified team.

Christ-centered possibilities far outweigh man-centered probabilities. Perhaps you need to get away in solitude for several days and ask your Savior to sear your soul with His goals. Think outside the box of small belief, for the Lord is unlimited in His abilities and resources. God-sized goals arrest your attention, adjust your attitude, and accelerate your actions.

So prayerfully set great goals, and He will grow your character in the process, while influencing others for His glory. Trust Him to teach you the way, to show you with eyes of faith way beyond the bounds of your experience, for His plan will prevail. The Bible says, "I know you can do all things; no plan of yours can be thwarted" (Job 42:2).

What goal is God giving me that I need to accept by faith and work hard towards its accomplishment?

Related Readings: Genesis 18:14; Jeremiah 32:17; Matthew 19:26; Ephesians 1:19-20

3

Mentor Young People

At the window of my house I looked out through the lattice. I saw among the simple, I noticed among the young men, a youth who lacked judgment.
Proverbs 7:6-7

Most young people yearn for someone to invest time and wisdom in them. They know deep in their heart they need help to handle heartaches. Their naïve knowledge has yet to graduate them from the school of hard knocks; so they need loving and wise instruction. Who in your circle of influence is a candidate for your caring attention?

It may be a son or daughter, a colleague at work, or a friend from church. God places people in our lives for a purpose. Perhaps you prayerfully pursue a mentor relationship with a teachable young person. He or she can learn from your mistakes as much or more as from your wise choices.

Mentors are not perfect, just wiser from failures and humbled by successes. Look around and ask the Lord to lead you to a young person who may be edging in the wrong direction. Reach out to that young person, and you will have returned the favor to someone who loved you.

Indeed, mentors take time for others because they are eternally grateful for those who took time for them. Gratitude to God is a great reason to go the extra mile with someone younger. Read books together, maybe a book a month for a year. Meet over coffee to discuss how the book challenged your thinking and changed your behavior for the better.

Young leaders can preclude problems when they are able to model the wise habits of their mentors. Always invite an older adult into your life who can educate you in the ways of God. Moreover, the mentor process is valuable to both parties. It provides accountability, encouragement, love, and obedience to Christ's commands. Mentor young people so they follow the right path, and in turn help someone else do the same.

The Bible says, "Encourage the young women to love their husbands, to love their children. Likewise urge the young men to be sensible" (Titus 2:4, 6 NASB).

Who is the young person in my life in whom the Lord is leading me to invest time, wisdom, and resources?

Related Readings: Job 32:6; Psalm 119:9; Matthew 28:20; Titus 2:1-8

4

Travel Temptations

"My husband is not at home; he has gone on a long journey. He took his purse filled with money and will not be home till full moon."
Proverbs 7:19-20

How do you deal with temptations when you travel? Conversely, what is your behavior when you are the spouse left at home? Is your house a palace of peace or a prison of confinement? Not only must the weary traveler be wary of wrong behavior, but so must the one left holding down the fort at home.

Perhaps as a couple you craft together guidelines defining what you will and will not do while separated by travel. Distance can grow the heart fonder and more faithful, or it can fire the flames of lust and infidelity. If you travel for your work, you most likely are motivated to meet the needs of your family.

However, every assignment is for a season; so maybe it is time to get off the road and reconnect with your child who is approaching the teenage years, or be there more often for your spouse who is starved for extra emotional support. Just be willing to adjust.

Moreover, do not drift into travel temptations that become divisive and deteriorate your marriage. One boundary may be to avoid bars and be back at your room soon after work and dinner. A righteous routine on the road gets the right results. When possible, make it a priority to travel with another person of similar values.

Be bold by becoming an influencer of integrity: good, clean fun without flirting with sin. On the other hand, your role in the marriage may be to daily support the children and manage the home. Take pride, not pity, during this season of unselfish service. By God's grace you are molding their minds to the things of Christ and to how they can influence the culture with His kingdom priorities.

You are as valuable as the one out working to provide for the family as you are working to preserve the family. Stay occupied in prayer, Bible study, and their school, and be available for those who need you. Marriage is a team effort that sees outstanding outcomes when you are both on the same page of love and obedience to Christ. Travel temptations are terminated on both ends through trust in the Lord and trust in each other.

The Bible says, "He trusts in the Lord; let the Lord rescue him. Let him deliver him, since he delights in him" (Psalm 22:8).

What behavior boundaries related to our time apart do I need to co-create with my spouse?

Related Readings: Numbers 5:11-15; Isaiah 46:6; Luke 12:39-46; 1 John 3:9

5

Unjust Treatment

When Jesus heard that John had been put in prison,
he withdrew to Galilee.
Matthew 4:12

There are days of mistreatment that come from disloyal and jealous people. Sometimes good people experience bad consequences so the glory of God can be made known through their lives. John boldly took a public stand for his faith and was punished for his courageous obedience to God. Do you feel like you have been wronged for doing right? Has your faith been put on trial, and were you convicted for speaking the truth?

Your circumstance of ill-treatment may not result in a physical rescue from Christ. It is in your trapped condition that He wants your intimacy with Him to grow deeper and sweeter. Your authorities at work may have broken a promise or used an unscrupulous process to get their desired results. You feel used and abused. So how will you respond? Will you return evil for evil, or will you extend grace in the face of extreme frustration?

"Do not repay anyone evil for evil.... 'If your enemy is hungry, feed him; if he is thirsty, give him something to drink. In doing this, you will heap burning coals on his head'" (Romans 12:17, 20). A radical response of love is a remedy for being isolated by an unjust person.

What are you learning as a result of feeling rejected or misunderstood? Has your determination grown in its resolve, and do you have more focused attention on the mission of the organization? Loss of freedom and/or resources aligns us back to the essentials of an effective strategy and efficient execution.

Use this time of limited options to build sustainable systems and the most productive processes. Cling to your core values as your compass for behavior. Your optimism is an insurgent against others' insecurities. Lastly, let the Lord be your source of strength. Faith forged on the anvil of adversity becomes solid steel in mental toughness, emotional stability, and spiritual maturity.

When people see Jesus in your humble, non-defensive attitude, they hear His voice of truth. Learn your lessons from the Lord during stressful situations, and leave it with Him to educate others in what needs to be done. Perseverance pays with respect and results.

Am I consumed with trusting Christ or with my unjust treatment? By God's grace, how can I love the unlovely?

Related Readings: Psalm 23; Psalm 109:5; 2 Timothy 3:2; Revelation 7:12

6

Christ's Calling

"'Come follow me,' Jesus said, 'and I will make you fishers of men.' At once they left their nets and followed him."
Matthew 4:19-20

Disciples of Jesus are called by the Lord to minister in their home and in the marketplace. However, Christ does call some of His followers to vocational ministry. It is a calling that many times comes to ordinary men and women who accomplish extraordinary results. Whom does He call? Christ's call comes to those who have a hungry heart for God.

Like Paul, you might have been suddenly smitten by a revelation of Jesus as Lord, or perhaps you were like David, who gradually went from feeding sheep what was perishable to feeding God's people the imperishable. Wherever Christ's calls, His first command is to love God and people. A calling without love is like a car without gasoline. It may be attractive on the outside, but it is not going anywhere. Thus, love large where the Lord has called you.

Furthermore, He has called you to endure hardships. "You have persevered and have endured hardships for my name, and have not grown weary" (Revelation 2:3). Christians are not immune to conflict; in fact, your faith at times invites difficulty. So do not seek to shelter your life from adversity, but rather position yourself in obedience to Christ's calling. It is out of your regular routine of serving Him that you will see what He has in store next.

Make sure you minister first to your spouse and children. Do not be like the cobbler who has no shoes for his family. Your creditability for Christ is seeing your faith lived out with those who know you the best. What does it profit a man if he saves the whole world and loses his family? A calling to family first frees you to evangelize and disciple with God's favor. His calling aligns with His commands; so service for Him is seamless.

Above all, the Lord is looking for those already engaged in His Word, growing in their character, and active in sharing their faith. His calling comes to Christians who desire the Holy Spirit to conform them into the image of Christ. Your humble imitation of Jesus comes out of your intimate walk with Him. He calls those whom He can trust. So do not look for your calling. Look for Christ, and He will reveal His calling to you.

"I, even I, have spoken; yes, I have called him. I will bring him, and he will succeed in his mission" (Isaiah 48:15).

What is Christ's calling for my life? Am I steadfast in loving the Lord and people?

Related Readings: Acts 9:10; 1 Corinthians 7:17; Hebrews 5:4; Revelation 7:14

7

Political Wisdom

"By me [wisdom] kings reign and rulers make laws that are just; by me princes govern, and all nobles who rule on earth."
Proverbs 8:15-16

The wisdom of God overshadows the best and brightest thinking of man. This is why our ancestors accessed the Almighty for knowledge and understanding in crafting our constitution. Its remarkable effectiveness is contingent on faith: faith in God, faith in government, and faith in its citizens.

Indeed, politicians who plead with Providence for wisdom will become the wiser. Those rulers who recognize their authority is from God will rule for God. There is a humble ambition that escorts the most effective statesman into public service, as political pride is exchanged for humble wisdom.

Those rule wisely in whom religion rules their conscience and character. Political wisdom is a prerequisite for those public servants who govern on behalf of the people and in alignment with the principles of Providence. These wise rulers are able to rest in peace in the middle of a storm.

A culture thrown into economic chaos especially needs principled men and women to step up, to sacrifice, and to make hard decisions. Wisdom in the middle of extreme uncertainty requires painful prescriptions to prevent further panic. Wise politicians face disastrous consequences and determine what is best for the whole in light of the long term.

Pray for political leaders to look beyond themselves and only short-term relief into the perspective and principles of God found in Holy Scripture. Indeed, political wisdom prays for intervention by the Almighty and understanding from the Almighty. Perhaps during desperate days a filibuster of faith is needed first; so our leaders start by looking and listening to the Lord.

Just laws follow political wisdom because they do what is right, as Christ defines right. Wise politicians keep their hand of faithfulness on the Bible's principles and their hearts submitted under the Lord's authority. Presidents honor Him by never forgetting their inaugural sacred vow of "So help me God."

The Bible says, "Blessed be the Lord your God who delighted in you to set you on the throne of Israel; because the Lord loved Israel forever, therefore He made you king, to do justice and righteousness" (1 Kings 10:9 NASB).

How can I facilitate political wisdom with those public servants in my circle of influence?

Related Readings: Psalm 148:11-13; Daniel 2:21-47; Romans 13:1; Revelation 19:11-16

8

Settle Matters

"Settle matters quickly with your adversary who is taking you to court. Do it while you are still with him on the way, or he may hand you over to the judge, and the judge may hand you over to the officer, and you may be thrown into prison."
Matthew 5:25

Settle matters sooner than later so all parties can focus on other significant issues. Lawsuits drain the life from relationships and can easily bring long-term relational harm. It is a financial, bottomless pit that throws stewardship to the wind. Check everyone's motivation; if fear, greed, or anger is driving the legal process, then it is unhealthy.

Why go through the emotional torture of a long, drawn-out, litigious process? A call for justice is legitimate, but can't there be a fair settlement without having to drag the relationship through an adversarial trial? Can't someone be the mature Christian adult and bring a close to the conflict? Money can be made again, but broken relationships may not be mended. Early Christians struggled with these issues of how to settle matters well.

"The very fact that you have lawsuits among you means you have been completely defeated already. Why not rather be wronged? Why not rather be cheated? Instead, you yourselves cheat and do wrong, and you do this to your brothers" (1 Corinthians 6:7-8).

Maybe you are in a legal contract that is onerous, even unbearable. Circumstances have changed in your work environment, and you are straddled with a commitment you are struggling to fulfill. Have you gone to the other party and explained your situation? Have you ask him for concessions and for a new contract? Perhaps there are other options that can be worked out between you? Humble yourself and trust God to work it out.

"My son, if you have put up security for your neighbor, if you have struck hands in pledge for another, if you have been trapped by what you said, ensnared by the words of your mouth, then do this, my son, to free yourself, since you have fallen into your neighbor's hands: Go and humble yourself; press your plea with your neighbor! Allow no sleep to your eyes, no slumber to your eyelids. Free yourself, like a gazelle from the hand of the hunter, like a bird from the snare of the fowler" (Proverbs 6:1-5).

Be honest, and from a prayerful position, seek to understand the needs of the other; then offer reasonable solutions to the situation. Pray the Lord will open the heart of the other party and bring creative alternatives to the table for discussion. Remember to keep your Christian testimony pure and attractive. Your kingdom is not of this world; so bring honor to King Jesus by doing the right thing in the right way. Settle matters soon.

How can I settle matters in a manner that honors the Lord and all parties?

Related Readings: Exodus 23:2-3; Hosea 10:4; 1 Corinthians 4:2-4; 1 Corinthians 6:1-6

Daily Wisdom in Your Inbox... A Free Subscription: www.wisdomhunters.com

9

Invite Instruction

"Rebuke a wise man and he will love you. Instruct a wise man and he
will be wiser still; teach a righteous man and
he will add to his learning."
Proverbs 9:8-9

Wise people invite instruction. They understand that correction and rebuke are necessary to grow in wisdom and righteous behavior. Without well-meaning instructors who are willing to get in our face, we only aspire to average at best. However, an invitation to mettle in my affairs defines authentic accountability.

Effective correction makes us uncomfortable at times, but we become all the wiser as a result. Indeed, conflict is inherent in accountability. So if your relationships are conflict free, you can bet you are not being held accountable in the truest sense. Wisdom comes in the form of raw relationships that reek with loving reproof and the willingness to change.

It is out of a rebuke that you wake up and understand the realities you are facing. Your spouse is not nagging, just nudging you to act responsibly. Therefore, invite instruction, and you will increase in wisdom and understanding. There are no regrets from wise recipients of reproof.

Furthermore, be willing to be the bearer of bad news. With love and grace, go to your friend who has asked for your counsel, and give him or her the truth. Pray first, and then deliver the unpleasant news. It is much better for others to see the error of their ways before they reach a point of no return. Talk to them, not about them.

Pray for them privately, not publically with a pious prayer request. It is a motivation of love that rebukes, and then it becomes a recipient of love. Your relationships will retreat in anger or rise to a higher level of respect through righteous rebuke. Take the time to prod another toward perfection because you care. Be respectful; instruct with patience, and one day the student may exceed the wisdom of the teacher.

Jesus said, "A student is not above his teacher, but everyone who is fully trained will be like his teacher" (Luke 6:40).

To whom do I need to listen in order to learn from their correction and rebuke?

Related Readings: Psalm 141:5; 2 Peter 3:18; 2 Timothy 4:2; Revelation 3:19

10

Beginning of Wisdom

"The fear of the Lord is the beginning of wisdom, and knowledge of the Holy One is understanding."
Proverbs 9:10

The fear of the Lord is fundamental to finding wisdom. Without awe of the Almighty, there is no access to His insights. Where reverence for His holiness is void, there is a lack of understanding into the ways of God. The first step in acquiring wisdom from almighty God is to fear Him. There is a worship of the Lord's majesty and a dread of His judgment.

His Holy Word—the Bible—is taken to heart as truth for the purpose of life transformation. At first, fear of the Lord may be so overwhelming that it casts out love and distracts our desire for intimacy. Anyone who has been broken understands this process. However, once a healthy fear of the Lord has been embraced, there is peace and knowledge of holy things because there is submission to and love for the Holy One.

Moreover, we mock God when we move away from the language of fear, but He is not one to be mocked. So as devoted followers of Christ, we sow the seeds of respect, reverence, and fear of the Lord. This discipline of faith results in a harvest of holiness, happiness, and wisdom. Fear of Him leads to knowledge of Him.

Therefore, bow before Him on your knees in prayer, and seek His face for forgiveness and relational restoration. Celebrate with Christ His conquest and ours over sin, sorrow, and death. What is counterintuitive on earth is intuitive in heaven. Listen to David admonish his son Solomon who became the wisest man in the world:

"As for you, my son Solomon, know the God of your father, and serve Him with a whole heart and a willing mind; for the Lord searches all hearts, and understands every intent of the thoughts. If you seek Him, He will let you find Him; but if you forsake Him, He will reject you forever" (1 Chronicles 28:9 NASB).

What area of my life lacks fear of the Lord, and how can I expose it to accountability?

Related Readings: Job 28:28; Psalm 111:10; Matthew 11:27; 1 John 5:20

11

Ill-gotten Treasures

Ill-gotten treasures are of no value, but righteousness
delivers from death.
Proverbs 10:2

Ill-gotten treasures insult integrity in the process of procuring profit. It is money manip-
ulated by man rather than blessed by God. There is no profit for the soul because the
means by which the money was made centered on self, not the Savior Jesus. He clearly addresses this: "For what will it profit a man if he gains the whole world and forfeits
his soul? Or what will a man give in exchange for his soul?" (Matthew 16:26 NASB).

Indeed, the methods and motives for making money matter. Can financial integrity be
assured without transparency in our business dealings or personal financial management? Does God wink at our wrongs when we attach aggressive giving to ill-gotten
gains? We need to be careful not to allow the ends of philanthropy to justify the means
of dishonesty.

However, honestly earned treasures place the hand of heaven on your head. You can
go to the bank and thank God along the way. So how do we know if our acquired treasures are legitimate as the Lord defines legitimate? One indicator is the extent of His
blessing because God blesses benevolence birthed out of brokenness and honest
work.

For example, you invite trustworthiness when there is full disclosure in financial report-
ing. It may mean losing a deal, but the Lord can lead you to better, even more lucra-
tive, opportunities. Moreover, treat others as you want to be treated. Jesus said, "Do
to others as you would have them do to you" (Luke 6:31). Thus, you avoid intimidation,
fear tactics, and disrespectful attitudes. God blesses respect.

Lastly, a company with a Christlike culture is attractive. You do not have to look over
your shoulder because you know other team members cover your back. Indeed, honesty is the best policy in producing profits. Untainted treasure comes from trusting
God. It matters as much how you make it as how you give it away.

The Bible says, "Make sure that your character is free from the love of money" (Hebrews 13:5 NASB).

Where is my character being tempted to compromise for the sake of cash, and how can I make sure I behave correctly?

Related Readings: Job 36:19; Psalm 49:6-10; Luke 12:15-21; James 5:1-3

12

God or Money

"No one can serve two masters. Either he will hate the one and love the other, or he will be devoted to the one and despise the other. You cannot serve both God and Money."
Matthew 6:24

How do you know if you love God or money more? Ask yourself if you worry more about missing your prayer time or missing your paycheck. Are you more anxious about what the Almighty thinks, or do you obsess over the opinion of others? Are you driven to seek God's kingdom first or to blindly build your own kingdom? Devotion to the eternal or the temporal is a choice. It cannot be to both. One really captures your worship.

Money makes promises it cannot keep, like security, peace, and prosperity. But the Lord makes promises He does keep, like grace, forgiveness, joy, and contentment. When the commands of these two contradict, will you follow Christ or cash? Decide now, so when you are in the emotion of the moment you do not give in to glittering gold.

What keeps you up at night? Is it how to make more money or how to make more of Jesus? Set your affections above, and you will be more effective below. The Lord is looking for His children with whom He can entrust more of His blessings. He longs for the faithful who use their finances to draw lost souls to salvation, hurting people to healing, and who boldly pray, "Your kingdom come ... on earth as it is in heaven" (Matthew 6:10).

Perhaps you take your family on a mission trip to see how the masses live with little money but with a lot of the Lord. It is revolutionary for a soul that has been seduced by the mistress of money to see how believers without stuff affectionately embrace their Lord and Savior Jesus. Expose your faith to the poor so you are liberated from wealth.

This is a heart issue. Who captures your affections—your Savior or your stuff? Money makes a poor master but a useful servant. Indeed, Jesus is the trustworthy Master with whom you can place your faith and devotion. Money tries to maneuver itself into a place of priority, but by faith you can relegate it to serve righteous causes. Love Him, not it.

"Do not love the world or anything in the world. If anyone loves the world, the love of the Father is not in him" (1 John 2:15).

What masters my mind and holds my heart—God or money? Who needs my money?

Related Readings: Malachi 3:8-10; Matthew 6:10; Colossians 3:1-10; 1 Timothy 6:6-10

13

Respectable Leaders

Now the overseer must be above reproach, the husband of but one
wife, temperate, self-controlled, respectable, hospitable, able to teach,
not given to drunkenness, not violent but gentle,
not quarrelsome, not a lover of money.
1 Timothy 3:2-3

Respectability invites respect. You may say, "I cannot get any respect." If so, on what do you base your expectations? Is it your charm, charisma, or ability to converse well? All of these do not mean you are respectable; in fact, they can repel respect and garner disrespect. Your skills and gifts require character to convene the admiration of others.

Respect is earned, not demanded. It is sustained by influence, not position. Presidents, preachers, and parents are given respect by their position, but if they consistently underperform or lack integrity, they lose respect. It is not a right of the irresponsible but a privilege of the dependable. Respectable leaders get right results in the right way.

Respectable leaders also rise to the occasion and do the right things. They persevere and provide stability instead of panicking and creating chaos. They take responsibility by espousing the values of the organization and by not gossiping and blaming others. There is a depth of character that runs deep within their soul, not to be stolen by sin.

Lastly, respectable leaders are well-thought-of when their track record is one of trustworthiness, honesty, and follow through. However, the goal is not for people to like you. They may not like you when you lovingly hold them accountable, but they will respect you. They may not like your discipline, but they will respect your consistency. They may not embrace your beliefs, but if expressed in humility, they will respect you. Perhaps you ask, "Am I respectable?" If so, you can expect respect.

The Bible says, "A sensible person wins admiration, but a warped mind is despised" (Proverbs 12:8 NTL).

What area of my character needs growth and transformation so as to solicit respect?

Related Readings: Exodus 18:21; Proverbs 15:27; John 10:12-13; Romans 16:18

14

Economic Storm

When the storm has swept by, the wicked are gone,
but the righteous stand firm forever.
Proverbs 10:25

Economic storms expose evil, like when the ocean tide goes out, you are able to see those in the water who are naked. Dead wood is swept away, to be seen no more. It may seem like the wicked are prospering, but eventually they will be found out. The Holy Spirit shakes out sin so it can be seen and judged. As the Lord promised His children in the past, "I will shake the house of Israel" (Amos 9:9).

What use is it to make a lot of noise and draw the attention of the elite and then lose your creditability under scrutiny? Economic storms collapse businesses and ministries that are dependent on debt and, conversely, cause good churches to increase in attendance. There is a purging of pride, and all manner of excess is exposed. What really matters in life becomes the priority: faith, family, friends, food, and shelter. Storms reveal worth.

Moreover, those who cling to Christ are not shaken. He is our cornerstone that no degree of chaos can challenge. The Bible says, "Those who trust in the Lord are like Mount Zion, which cannot be shaken but endures forever" (Psalm 125:1). The righteous cannot be moved because their Master is immovable. Therefore, stand firm in the Lord.

Furthermore, your stability in your Savior is security for your family, friends, and work associates. Your unwavering faith during difficult days helps them replace panic with peace, fear with faith, and compromise with conviction. Indeed, if all you have left is a firm foundation of faith, begin rebuilding God's big vision. Are you a wise builder?

Jesus says, "Therefore everyone who hears these words of mine and puts them into practice is like a wise man who built his house on the rock" (Matthew 7:24).

How can I build my life, home, and work on the solid rock of Jesus?

Related Readings: Job 20:5; Psalm 37:10; Acts 2:25; Hebrews 12:28

15

Possessions Complicate

Their possessions were so great that they were not able
to stay together. And quarreling arose.
Genesis 13:6-7

Abram and Lot had a lot of stuff. They were blessed with family, friends, and finances. However, things became complicated, and they were unable to coexist with each another. Though they needed one another, they could not stay with one another.

The fear of losing their possessions superseded the joy of growing their relationship. So they divided, and as a result of their vulnerability, Lot lost everything. Jesus said, "[A] household divided against itself will not stand" (Matthew 12:25).

Possessions are not wrong in themselves. However, when the management of your wealth compromises your loyalty to people, there is a problem. Possessions should be subservient to people; otherwise, things get out of kilter. People know if you value your net worth over them. So how do we keep this balance between possessions and people?

Begin with an inventory of your time. How do you spend your time? Do you spend more time in managing your stuff or loving on people? You may need to sell some of your property, or, better yet, give it away. If your possessions have priority over people, there is a problem.

Ask yourself, "Does my stuff compete with my relationship with God?" Perhaps you downsize your stuff so you can upsize your focus on your Savior Jesus. By God's grace, use the material fortune He has entrusted to you as a magnet that draws you closer to God and people. Use your blessing of discretionary time to bless others.

The Bible says, "Command those who are rich in this present world not to be arrogant nor to put their hope in wealth, which is so uncertain, but to put their hope in God, who richly provides us with everything for our enjoyment. Command them to do good, to be rich in good deeds, and to be generous and willing to share. In this way they will lay up treasure for themselves as a firm foundation for the coming age, so that they may take hold of the life that is truly life" (1 Timothy 6:17-19).

How can I position my possessions so the Lord possesses more of me and my family?

Related Readings: Genesis 36:6-7; Ecclesiastes 5:10-11; Luke 3:11; 2 Corinthians 9:6-15

16

Faithful Guide

The integrity of the upright guides them, but the unfaithful are
destroyed by their duplicity.
Proverbs 11:3

Integrity is an instrument of almighty God. He uses it to guide His children in the direction He desires for them. Have you ever wondered what God would have you do? Integrity is His directive to do the next right thing and trust Him with the results. It is out of our honesty we begin to comprehend Christ's desires. He delights in our uprightness.

For example, are you totally honest on your tax return? Is your tax preparer a person of unquestionable integrity? We can trust professionals to represent us well, but we are ultimately responsible for honest outcomes. Furthermore, is there anything you are doing, if printed as a newspaper headline, which would embarrass you and your family? Indeed, integrity brings joy to heaven and security on earth. It is your guide for godly living.

Moreover, the iniquity of the unfaithful destroys. The blessing of God is removed as it cannot be bought with bad behavior. Relationships are scarred, and some even severed, over dishonest dealings. Overnight, poor judgment can soil and potentially destroy a hard-earned reputation. Pride acts like integrity is only for others. It deceives itself and becomes a disgrace for its dishonest and duplicitous ways. Iniquity is an unfaithful guide.

"I put in charge of Jerusalem my brother Hanani, along with Hananiah the commander of the citadel, because he was a man of integrity and feared God more than most people do" (Nehemiah 7:2).

So we ask ourselves, "How can I be a man or woman of integrity over the balance of my life?" There is plainness about those who base their behavior on the principles of God's Word—nothing fancy, only faithful living in their daily routine. The grace of God governs their soul, the truth of God renews their mind, and accountability is an anchor for their actions. Honestly ask yourself, "Is integrity my faithful guide?"

The Bible says, "May integrity and uprightness protect me, because my hope is in you" (Psalm 25:21).

How can I better integrate integrity as a guide for my business dealings and behavior at home?

Related Readings: Genesis 20:4-7; Hosea 13:9; Matthew 7:13; Romans 7:9-12

17

Follow Jesus First

When Jesus saw the crowd around him, he gave orders to cross to the other side of the lake. Then a teacher of the law came to him and said, "Teacher, I will follow you wherever you go."
Matthew 8:18-19

Good leaders are first good followers. Do you follow the orders of Jesus? When He asks you to do the uncomfortable, do you move out of your comfort zone with confidence? Compelling Christian leaders have a focused following on their Master, the Lord Jesus. Where is He asking you to go that requires sacrifice and unconditional commitment? His orders do not always make sense, but they are totally trustworthy and helpful.

When He directs you to leave the noise of the crowds to the quietness of a few, do not delay. If you are obsessed by activity, you can easily lose your edge on energy and faith. When all my oomph is consumed on serving every request and answering every call, I have no time or concentration to hear from Christ. What is He saying? This is the most important inquiry I can make. What is Jesus telling me to do? When I listen, I learn.

You may be in the middle of a monster season of success; so make sure your achievements do not muffle the Lord's message. It is when we are fast and furious that our faith becomes perfunctory and predictable. Leadership requires alone time to retool and recalibrate our character. People follow when they know you have been with Jesus.

The most difficult part may be the transition from doing less to listening and thinking more. If you as the leader are not planning ahead, who is? Who has the best interest of the enterprise in mind? Who is defending the mission and vision of the organization so there is not a drift into competing strategies? Follow Jesus first; then He frees you to see.

Where is the Lord leading you to go? Will you lag behind with excellent excuses, or will you make haste and move forward by faith? Go with God, and He will direct you through the storms of change. He may seem silent at times, but remember He led you to this place, and where He leads, He provides. Follow Jesus first, and go wherever He goes. You will lose people in the process, but you will gain better people for His next phase.

"Then Jesus said to his disciples, 'If anyone would come after me, he must deny himself and take up his cross and follow me'" (Matthew 16:24).

Where is Jesus leading me to go? Am I willing to let go and trust Him with what is next?

Related Readings: Numbers 32:11; Isaiah 8:10-12; 1 Corinthians 1:11-13; Revelation 14:4

18

Stability's Influence

"Stay in this land for a while, and I will be with you and will bless you."
Genesis 26:3

Your investment in one geographical location compounds your influence over time. This is important because it affects your family, your community, and your career. It benefits your family to stay in one place because it gives them security and the opportunity to build lifelong friendships.

Over time the community around your family becomes a built-in accountability. You get to know the values and priorities of people, and they get to know yours. You watch out for each other's children, and you are more accountable. This high level of trust and expectation comes over time and is invaluable.

Your career creditability is enhanced if you stay in one place. People grow to love and trust you. They see you as reliable, someone they can go to with a need or question. They know you can get an answer or a referral of a helpful resource. So what type of location should you decide to put down roots with a goal to influence others for Christ?

Pray for an area where you and your family can grow spiritually. This means you have the opportunity to develop community and attend church with like-minded believers. This is critical; otherwise, you miss the opportunity for encouragement, mentorship, and accountability. This can happen in college, on your first work assignment, on the mission field, or in the area where you grew up. Early in life, look for those who can become lifelong mentors for you; as you get older, look for those you can mentor.

God blesses long-term relational commitments. This takes trust. For example, it may mean turning down a raise and not moving, but you know in your heart by staying put your family and marriage will be stronger.

Yes, there is a time to move and a time to stay. Bridle your appetite for more and more material wealth, keep your life simple, and trust God in one location. Over time your influence will compound, and relationally you will become filthy rich. Are you content to leverage your influence for Christ?

The Bible says, "Remember your leaders, who spoke the word of God to you. Consider the outcome of their way of life and imitate their faith" (Hebrews 13:7).

Am I developing relationships for the long term so I can earn the right to influence them for Christ?

Related Readings: Exodus 32:13; Psalm 37:1-6; Philippians 4:9; Hebrews 11:9-16

19

Time to Go

By faith Abraham, when called to go to a place he would later receive
as his inheritance, obeyed and went, even though he did not know
where he was going.
Hebrews 11:8

It is time to go when God says so, even though you are not sure where you are going. Abraham was "a friend of God" (James 2:23 NASB) who trusted the heart of God. He was secure in his faith, knowing his heavenly Father would not lead him astray. Are you okay with only the call of Christ as your next step? Is He calling you out of your comfort zone to a new level of faith and obedience? It is here that you hear Him quite clearly.

Maybe He wants you to move with your company so your career can become the means of funding your passion for missions. Locals in a foreign country are keenly interested in visitors to their world who are teachers, housewives, doctors, bankers, and businessmen. The marketplace is your ministry. It validates your value and confirms your character. The Lord will use your obedience to encourage the faith of others and especially the faith of your family.

The faith of parents often procures the blessing of obedience on their posterity. When your teenage son sees you say yes to Christ's challenge, he is more likely to say yes to wisdom when he is faced with issues of trust. Your daughter will not soon forget your family's earnest prayers as you sought to see God's best and obey. Parents who obey God's call create the same expectation for their children; so follow the Lord for them.

Lastly, the call of Christ leads to His blessing on earth and in heaven. It may mean prosperity. It may mean poverty. Or it may mean somewhere in between. The most important reward is that of your eternal inheritance. Leave a legacy of loving the Lord, and you will have loved your children. Follow Him faithfully, and there is a much higher probability they will as well. Is it time to go? Then go with your best friend Jesus.

The Bible says, "God's intimate friendship blessed my house" (Job 29:4).

Where is Christ calling me to a higher level of faith and obedience?

Related Readings: Nehemiah 9:7-8; Psalm 105:6-11; Acts 7:2-4; Galatians 3:6

20

False Trust

Whoever trusts in his riches will fall, but the righteous
will thrive like a green leaf.
Proverbs 11:28

Trust in stuff will cause you to stumble and eventually fall. Why? Why is money unfit for trust? It is unreliable because it cannot save us or bring us forgiveness, peace, and contentment. Money is an unemotional master that can trip you up if it becomes the basis for your security. It can be here today and gone tomorrow. Money moves around like a gypsy looking for the next place to live. Those who lose their focus on Christ and instead trust in riches will fall.

The Bible says, "Cast but a glance at riches, and they are gone, for they will surely sprout wings and fly off to the sky like an eagle" (Proverbs 23:5). Trust in riches causes some to fall from the faith because they equate wealth with success. However, you can be faithful to the Lord and thus be successful whether rich or poor. It may take our losing money to reveal our true motivations. Trust in riches is a recipe for false security, fear, and sadness.

However, the righteous understand that the role of riches is to remind them of God's provision. The Bible says, "Moreover, when God gives any man wealth and possessions, and enables him to enjoy them, to accept his lot and be happy in his work—this is a gift of God" (Ecclesiastes 5:19). Are you struggling with the reduction of your wealth? Do you remember what really mattered when you were first married? Was it trust in the Lord, your spouse, and good health? The righteous thrive in trust and obedience to Christ.

Lastly, guard your good name during a financial crisis. Character is of much greater value than cash. The Bible says, "A good name is more desirable than great riches; to be esteemed is better than silver or gold" (Proverbs 22:1). This means you do not fear, and you follow through with your commitments. Faith grows in its giving during uncertain times. Am I thriving or surviving? Is my trust in gold or God?

Where does the Lord want me to aggressively give money so that I know my trust is in Him?

Related Readings: Deuteronomy 8:12-14; Job 31:24-25; Matthew 13:22; 1 Timothy 6:17

21

Routine Work

He who works his land will have abundant food, but he who chases
fantasies lacks judgment.
Proverbs 12:11

Routine work may not be sexy, but it is necessary. It is necessary to meet our needs
and the needs of those who depend on us. The same work, day in and day out, can
seem simple and even boring, but it is a test of our faithfulness. Will I continue to faithfully carry out uncomplicated responsibilities, even when my attention span is suffer-
ing? If so, this is God's path to blessing: "Steady plodding brings prosperity" (Proverbs
21:5 TLB).

The contrast to routine work is chasing after phantom deals that are figments of our
imagination. Be careful not to be led astray by fantasies that lead nowhere. It is false
faith to think a gimmick or some conniving circumstance can replace hard work.
Wisdom stops chasing after the next scheme and sticks instead to the certainty of
available work. What does your spouse say is the smart thing to do? Give your spouse
all the facts, and listen.

Furthermore, work is easily carried out when everything is going well and there are no
indicators of job loss or an increase in responsibilities with less pay. However, it is during these uncertain times that Christ followers can step up and set the example. Your
attitude of hope and hard work is a testimony of trust in the Lord. Stay engaged in exe-
cuting your tasks with excellence, and you will inspire others to their labor of love.

Lastly, see routine work as your worship of the Lord. He is blessing your faithfulness to
follow through with the smallest of details. Are you content to serve Christ in your current career?

The Bible says, "Whatever you do, work at it with all your heart, as working for the Lord,
not for men, since you know that you will receive an inheritance from the Lord as a
reward. It is the Lord Christ you are serving" (Colossians 3:23-24).

Is my work a compelling testimony to the excellence of God's gracious work?

Related Readings: Genesis 2:15; 1 Kings 19:19; Romans 12:11; 1 Timothy 4:11-12

22

Diligence Rules

Diligent hands will rule, but laziness ends in slave labor.
Proverbs 12:24

How hard do you work, or do you hardly work? God said to Adam, "Cursed is the ground because of you; through painful toil you will eat of it all the days of your life. By the sweat of your brow you will eat your food" (Genesis 3:17, 19). And He explained to Moses, "Six days you shall labor and do all your work, but the seventh day is a Sabbath to the Lord your God. On it you shall not do any work" (Exodus 20:9-10).

Has our culture become accustomed to receiving good things without great effort? Who is entitled to influence without being industrious? Perhaps there is a dearth of diligence that has depressed people and economies. Laziness leads to the control of others, while honest labor is given opportunities and advancement. Do not despair in your diligence, for you are set up for success. Mind your business meticulously, and you will enjoy the business.

Indeed, intense industry leads to preferment. The Bible says, "Now the man Jeroboam was a valiant warrior, and when Solomon saw that the young man was industrious, he appointed him over all the forced labor of the house of Joseph" (1 Kings 11:28 NASB). Your faithfulness to your work is not going unnoticed. Your diligence is a distinctive that separates you from the average or lazy laborer. Security comes with this level of service.

Lastly, the Lord blesses hands that are hard at work. He smiles when He sees your service exceeds expectations. You go the extra mile to make sure others are cared for, just as you would like to be treated. Because of your thoroughness on the job and your integrity in its execution, God knows you can be trusted with more.

The Bible says, "The elders who direct the affairs of the church well are worthy of double honor, especially those whose work is preaching and teaching" (1 Timothy 5:17).

Does my work honor the Lord with its focused diligence and commitment to quality?

Related Readings: 1 Kings 12:20; Proverbs 10:4; Romans 12:8; 1 Timothy 4:15

23

Brutal Facts

Then Joab went into the house of the king and said, "Today you have humiliated all your men, who have just saved your life and the lives of your sons and daughters and the lives of your wives and concubines."
2 Samuel 19:5

Brutal facts are not always pretty or inviting, but they are reality. Initially, brutal news may take you back and even make you feel beat-up. But take heart; it is good for bad news to travel fast. You are better off to hear negative news first, before the information becomes filtered through other perspectives or the facts fester and become worse.

Brutal facts that are not given attention move from an inflamed infection to relational and organizational gangrene. Inevitably, there follows an amputation; someone or something has to be severed. This extreme action could have been avoided if the brutal facts had been revealed, recognized, and acted upon. Brutal facts are our friends. So do not dismiss the messenger because the message is bad; he or she is just the delivery person.

Yes, the messenger's attitude and character may not always be stellar, but the content of his or her words can be extremely accurate. The wise receiver of brutal facts will extract the chaff and keep the wheat. Brutal facts may mean you have lost touch with those who love you the most. In your zeal to provide for them, you have failed to get to know them.

A brutal fact may relate to your finances. What is the reality of your cash situation? Come clean with your spouse, and seek accountability from a trusted third party. Or the state of your physical health may be a heart attack waiting to happen. Take care of your "temple," or it will take care of you by tumbling down around you. Do you rationalize that all of your activity is for the Lord? The truth is that He can get by just fine without any of us.

So where can we find these brutal facts? Your spouse, parent, or friend is a good starting point. They have a vested interest in you; so normally their perception of the facts is fairly accurate. Listen with an ear to learn, but if you become defensive or argumentative, they will eventually shut down. Because they care is why they want you to be aware.

Why not change on your own terms rather than being forced to change on the terms of another? This is the essence of brutal facts—there are some things that need to change. You, the work culture, your family are always in flux; so use this as an opportunity to move from mediocrity to excellence. Embrace the brutal facts, learn from them, and become better.

"Then Nathan said to David, 'You are the man! This is what the Lord, the God of Israel, says'" (2 Samuel 12:7).

Who currently has concerns that I need to seriously consider? How do I need to change?

Related Readings: 2 Kings 5:10; Haggai 1:13; Romans 9:1; 3 John 1:12-13

24

Preparation's Provision

"I will provide for you there, because five years
of famine are still to come."
Genesis 45:11

Because Joseph prepared, he was able to provide. He provided for his family and for an entire nation. His preparations were very focused, deliberate, and timely. For seven years he was diligent to save during the days of abundance so there would be provision for all during the days of leanness. Yes, God provides, but usually through our wise decisions and/or someone else's. God does not operate in a vacuum. He works through people.

He wants us to prepare so we can be in a position to provide for others and for ourselves. Life is one big preparation. How are you doing in your preparations? How are your spiritual preparations? Are you prepared relationally? Do you currently spend time in your physical preparations? What are you doing about your career preparations? Are you preparing financially for the future?

"Finish your outdoor work and get your fields ready; after that, build your house" (Proverbs 24:27).

Consider your financial preparations. "The wise man saves for the future, but the foolish man spends whatever he gets" (Proverbs 21:20 TLB). Consistent and steady saving prepares you for the future. Let a budget be your guide. Short-term restraint will allow you to enjoy long-term provision.

The day will come when your wise preparations will provide for you, and they may position you to provide for others. God does provide, but He usually works through wise preparation. "Righteousness goes before him and prepares the way for his steps" (Psalm 85:13).

Lastly, the focus of spiritual preparation is eternity. Your time, money, and resources are invested in the kingdom for the sake of eternity. The disciplines of renewing our minds with God's Word, trusting in Him through prayer, giving generously, and loving others to Christ build our spiritual muscles.

Relational preparation is investment in people. It is the ability to forgive fast and the unselfishness to freely connect others with your relationships and resources. Am I using my relational influence to point others to Christ? "A voice of one calling: 'In the desert prepare the way for the Lord; make straight in the wilderness a highway for our God'" (Isaiah 40:3).

What preparation is required before I take the next of faith in the Lord's will?

Related Readings: Proverbs 6:6-8; Amos 4:12; 2 Timothy 2:21; Revelation 21:2

25

Skill and Ability

"See, I have chosen Bezalel ... and I have filled him with the Spirit of God, with skill, ability and knowledge in all kinds of crafts."
Exodus 31:2-3

Our ability to work comes from God. Our ability to earn a degree and make money comes from God. Our ability to paint, sing, play a musical instrument, and execute a deal comes from God. He calls us and He equips us to carry out His will for our lives. Where He calls, He equips. And yes, if you do not use the God-given abilities you have, you could lose them.

You could lose them because of poor stewardship or a bad testimony. You could lose your skills because of atrophy. Just as muscle shrinks and becomes useless without use, so do the skills, abilities, gifts, and knowledge given to us by God. How are you doing in the management of your God-given abilities? His expectations are for you to continue to grow and improve. He wants you to focus on the things you do the very best.

"There are different kinds of gifts, but the same Spirit distributes them. There are different kinds of service, but the same Lord. There are different kinds of working, but in all of them and in everyone it is the same God at work" (1 Corinthians 12:4-6).

As we mature, ideally we narrow our focus to the one thing that is effortless for us. This is the thing that others say we do best and that blesses them when they are around us. Position your life to do the one thing at which you have become a genius by God's grace. It may be teaching; then focus on teaching. It may be leading; then focus on leading. It may be coaching; then focus on coaching. It may be singing; then focus on singing. It may be parenting; then focus on parenting. It may be writing; then focus on writing.

This requires discipline and in some cases sacrifice, but trust God with who you are. Serve out of your sweet spot so you and everyone around you will be blessed. Yes, there are economic considerations, but each stage of life has its own opportunities. Stay nimble and seize each opportunity in the context of what you do best, and never forget to give God the credit for your abilities.

"Therefore I remind you to stir up the gift of God which is in you through the laying on of my hands" (2 Timothy 1:6 NKJV).

Prayer: "Heavenly Father, thank you for gifting me to accomplish Your will, keep me growing and learning in my skills and abilities."

Related Readings: Deuteronomy 33:11; Proverbs 22:29; John 3:27; 1 Corinthians 12:4-11

26

Preparation Precedes Power

"This is the one about whom it is written: 'I will send my messenger ahead of you, who will prepare your way before you.'"
Matthew 11:10

Jesus spent thirty years in private preparation for three years of public service. He knew the necessary need to wait on His heavenly Father for the power of His blessing before He embarked on His eternal mission. What passionate desire has the Lord laid on your heart that awaits your thorough preparation? Like Elijah, you first prepare an altar of sacrifice by faith and wait on God to send forth His fire from heaven to ignite your work.

Similar to Jesus, you probably depend on others as part of your preparation process. The creditability of John the Baptist paved the way for the Lamb of God. In the same way, the good reputation of trusted friends can accelerate your success. This is why it is wise to wait on the endorsement of other trusted leaders. Pay the price of being mentored before you run ahead to your next assignment. New leaders need the approval of the former leaders.

Pain is another product of preparation. Until your perspective has been seasoned by adversity, your confidence has not been tempered away from arrogance and toward humility. God does not waste pain as it produces the character required to represent Christ. It is in our hurt that we cry out in humble dependence, confession, and repentance. We learn the good and bad about ourselves in pain's process. Pain produces patience.

Are you expecting to receive the fruit of preparation without paying the price to prepare? Ministers who prepare are endowed with power from on high. Preparation precedes anointing. Parents who prepare learn from experienced parents. Preparation precedes obedient children. Students who prepare privately are recognized publically. Preparation precedes education. Leaders who prepare their minds and hearts feel God's favor.

What is your next step in the process of preparation? Is it to silently serve the poor or to boldly challenge the rich? Is it to earnestly work with your hands so you can better relate with your head? Do not dismiss thorough preparation in place of zealous short-cuts. Stay the course in Christ's school of learning submission, as His power rests on the prepared.

"'Answer me, O Lord, answer me, so these people will know that you, O Lord, are God, and that you are turning their hearts back again.' Then the fire of the Lord fell and burned up the sacrifice, the wood, the stones and the soil, and also licked up the water in the trench. When all the people saw this, they fell prostrate and cried, 'The Lord—he is God! The Lord—he is God!'" (1 Kings 18:37-39).

What patient preparation do I need to complete? Am I serving others in God's power?

Related Readings: Psalm 85:13; Amos 4:12; Ephesians 4:12; 2 Timothy 2:21

27

Willing to Accept

"And if you are willing to accept it, he is the Elijah who was to come."
Matthew 11:14

Hard words, hard people, and hard situations are hard to accept. Do you or someone you know feel like you are between a rock and a hard spot? Do your options seem like they have dried up? Is your energy to press forward depleted? Perhaps it is time to accept the cold, hard facts of where you find yourself. Reality has a way of catching up with our denial.

It is okay to be optimistic, but not to the peril of ignoring your predicament. Are emotional reactions driving your decision making, or do you prayerfully process the facts clearly and objectively with wise input from others you trust? Do you need to give up something—your house, your car, your career, your travel, or your expectations? What is the Lord asking you to give up so that you can gain Him and His peace? Acceptance requires action.

Furthermore, there are people to accept who require additional patience and grace. Have others wronged you to the point that your resentment is blocking your acceptance of them? You may justify your rejection of them because of their rejection of you. For example, children and parents can let us down and even devastate us, but Christians do not have the option of not accepting them for who they are. Love accepts even unworthy recipients.

Do you find yourself in a situation where you do not feel accepted—a new job, in-laws, a new school, a new city, a new relationship? You can stew in self-pity, or you can take the initiative to reach out to your rejecters. Kindness reaches out and rejects rejection. "A man who has friends must himself be friendly" (Proverbs 18:24 NKJV).

Above all, are you willing to accept God's call on your life? When His will is uncomfortable and uncertain, will you still go there in trust? Start by accepting Christ by faith as your Savior and Lord, and then continue to accept His commands as evidence that you are His disciple. Acceptance of the Lord allows you to love Him and other people. Acceptance cannot continue alone but is accelerated and accompanied by the Almighty's grace and love.

Do I wholeheartedly accept God's plan for my life? Whom do I need to accept in love?

Related Readings: Genesis 4:7; Ecclesiastics 5:19; Romans 11:15; 1 Timothy 1:15

28

Dollar Cost Averaging

*Dishonest money dwindles away, but he who gathers
money little by little makes it grow.*
Proverbs 13:11

Is there a method to your money management? Do you have a process in place to steadily save over time? If not, it is never too late to set up a system for saving. Some of us struggle with this because we bet on big returns, only to suffer loss. Steadily saving is not sexy but secure. Finances can be an elusive enemy or a friend who has our back.

Get-rich-quick schemes only feed greed. In God's economy, it is those who diligently deposit smaller amounts in a secure place who reap rewards. It is wise wealth that makes the first 10 percent of their income a gift offering in the form of a tithe to their heavenly Father and the second 10 percent an investment in their future. Money obtained by vanity is spent on vanity, but money gained by hard work and honesty is retained for growth.

It does take discipline not to spend all our earnings in an instant. Commercials and our obligation as consumers exploit our emotions. Culture sucks us in to spend not all we have but more than we have; so be on guard with a simple system for savings. For example, set up an automatic draft from each paycheck that goes straight into a savings account. Preserve this cash, and one day your financial fruit tree will become an orchard.

Lastly, look to the Lord as your provider, and see yourself as a steward of His stuff. The management of your Master's money requires savings. God's desire is growth in your financial security so you are free to give more and serve others. So we ask ourselves, "Am I frivolously spending just for today, or am I disciplined each day to deposit a dollar toward tomorrow?"

"The plans of the diligent lead to profit as surely as haste leads to poverty" (Proverbs 21:5).

What is a wise plan for me to systematically save as a responsible follower of Jesus?

Related Readings: Psalm 128:2; Jeremiah 17:11; Ephesians 4:28; James 5:1-5

29

Practical Provision

At that time Jesus went through the grainfields on the Sabbath. His
disciples were hungry and began to pick
some heads of grain and eat them.
Matthew 12:1

The Lord's provision does not lack in practicality. What need do you have? Are you
stressed out by striving, or have you looked around for a simple solution? It may take
some creativity and risk, but if Christ has what you need in close proximity, do not be
shy. Forgo ego, and appropriate faith. Access His provision, and let Him manage your
image. His provision may not be positive for public relations, but He knows what is
best.

Is your struggle over lack of work? Are you willing to work with your hands outside of
your interests to provide for your family? Labor is labor; it can be toilsome and tiring at
times. So even if your job is temporarily tedious, look at it as a gift from God. Be proud
of your work, even when it is more transactional than relational. Our perspective
becomes more grateful and realistic when work becomes a necessity, not an option.

Productive work keeps us focused on provision for those who depend on us, and it
keeps us away from unproductive activities. Paul states it well, "For even when we
were with you, we gave you this rule: 'If a man will not work, he shall not eat.' We hear
that some among you are idle. They are not busy; they are busybodies" (2
Thessalonians 3:10-11). Provision follows preparation; so prepare your heart in humility, your head in integrity, and your hands in diligence. God helps those who prepare,
work hard, and trust Him.

It is bad theology to blame God, the church, and others for our needy situation. It is
good theology to be resourceful and seek out solutions that require humility and focus.
Whom have you invested in over the years who would be honored to give back to you?
When you are transparent about your needs, you give other souls an opportunity to be
blessed by blessing you. Honesty is a pure platform to invite God's provision through
friends.

Lastly, do not allow religious restraints to rob you from receiving mercy and being served on the Christian Sabbath. Is there a better time for the body of Christ to care for one another than on our day of corporate worship and biblical teaching? Indeed, engage with believers when you are in need; each part of the body needs the other. If you remain silent, you deny others a blessing; when you speak up, God practically provides.

"But God has combined the members of the body and has given greater honor to the parts that lacked it, so that there should be no division in the body, but that its parts should have equal concern for each other. If one part suffers, every part suffers with it; if one part is honored, every part rejoices with it" (1 Corinthians 12:24-26).

Have I recognized and received God's provision? Who needs my provision?

Related Readings: Joshua 9:14; Proverbs 6:8; Romans 5:17; 1 Timothy 6:17

30

Leadership in Adversity

After that, he poured water into a basin and began to wash his disciples' feet, drying them with the towel that was wrapped around him.
John 13:5

Adversity invites leaders to lead. It is your time to trust the Lord and lead by faith, not fear. In hard times a leader asks, "Will I panic or pray?" "Will I stay calm or be sucked into the chaos?" "Will I serve the team or stay secluded in silence?" Jesus faced death, but He was determined to stay focused on His heavenly Father and the mission at hand. Adversity is an opportunity to prove the point of Providence. Christ is in control.

How can you use adversity to your advantage as a leader? One way is to unify the team around common objectives and goals. There is no better way to bring people together than in the fires of hardship and difficulty. In fact, you probably will not succeed without the team rising to its next level of leadership and team support. So reward creativity because limitations lead to innovation. Lead the team to accomplish more with less. Paul said, "We put no stumbling block in anyone's path, so that our ministry will not be discredited. Rather, as servants of God we commend ourselves in every way: in great endurance; in troubles, hardships and distresses" (2 Corinthians 6:3-4).

Moreover, use hard times to create a culture of hard work and honesty. It may mean longer hours and less pay, but sacrifice is the price to be paid for productivity. Invite honest feedback so you accurately and effectively improve process and products. Raise team expectations beyond just surviving to thriving. They look to you for leadership; so lead.

Lastly, serve at home and work with appreciation. It is easy to demand more and more under pressure and forget to say "Thank you." Perhaps you give the team a day off, leave a grateful voicemail, buy everyone lunch, or send flowers. Wise leaders honestly inquire, "How can I out serve others, especially in the face of misfortune?" "Where do I need to take responsibility and not blame outside forces?" Leaders model the way.

Jesus said, "I have set you an example that you should do as I have done for you" (John 13:15).

Prayer: "Heavenly Father, I need You in the good times and in the bad times. Give me hope, humility and grace to persevere as Your servant leader."

Related Readings: Exodus 4:28-30; 1 Samuel 17:22-24; Acts 10:4-8

31

Eternal Optimist

So we fix our eyes not on what is seen, but on what is unseen. For what is seen is temporary, but what is unseen is eternal.
2 Corinthians 4:18

Eternal optimists base their optimism on the eternal, not the temporal. The temporal is consumed with current circumstances, while the eternal experiences eternal security. The temporal is anxious about another adverse event, while the eternal is at peace with Providence. The temporal trusts what it can see, while the eternal trusts in the unseen. Do you glance at the temporal and gaze on the eternal? If so, you are an eternal optimist.

By faith we see the Lord who is unseen, and this is what compels us to obey Christ. Moses experienced this during a time of transition. "By faith he left Egypt, not fearing the king's anger; he persevered because he saw him who is invisible" (Hebrews 11:27). Your eternal optimism is what gives you the courage to carry on; so do not let temporal pessimists persuade you to lose heart. Stay fixed on your Savior, the author of your faith.

Eternal optimism exits when fear gets the upper hand. Fear seeks to flush out your faith as irresponsible and irrelevant. However, it is faith that keeps you grounded in God, the definer of reality. The righteous learn to live in the reality of the Lord's love and leadership. Pain and striving are temporary, but healing and peace are eternal. You can be optimistic, knowing by faith you can be certain of the unseen.

"Now faith is being sure of what we hope for and certain of what we do not see" (Hebrews 11:1).

Lastly, are you a temporal pessimist or an eternal optimist? Are you striving to survive or thriving to succeed? Look to the unseen, and you will one day understand. Engage with the Almighty's agenda, and your focus will be forever and your results eternally significant. Can your family and friends depend on you to be an eternal optimist? Your hopeful attitude in the eternal gives them reason to be optimists. Live and exclaim out loud, "There is surely a future hope for you, and your hope will not be cut off" (Proverbs 23:18).

Where is God calling me to see, with eyes of faith, the unseen, eternal optimism of Jesus?

Related Readings: Psalm 73:26; Isaiah 51:10-11; Matthew 6:21; John 6:27

N O T E S

NOTES

WHAT READERS ARE SAYING ABOUT WISDOM HUNTERS

Skill and Ability
Thank you for reminding us to stir up the gifts that God has given us. May He help us to focus on the ones that are of Him. May we always remember that every good gift and every perfect gift comes from God. May God bless you and the work you do for Him. – Deborah

The Lord's Name
This has GOT to be one of the MOST inspiring devotionals I have read in a long time. Thank you so much for the devotionals we are able to read online. God bless you. – Jill

Alive and Well
Wow! I don't know if it can be conveyed any sweeter or any plainer than that! Thank You, Jesus! – Dudley

Shameless Audacious Prayers
Thanks so much for this wisdom of truth. Sometimes I am weary of all the requests for things but not for God. For me this is a keeper to be looked at and read until I know it by heart. Thank you! – Ken

God Is Working
I really appreciate the reading for today. I know God is in control, but I always forget it. This spoke to me today in a way I have not experienced before. – Jen

For a Season
Your message today really blessed my heart. It is a confirmation of where God has me. This is but a season for me, and sometimes it is difficult for us to recognize when we are in a season. Your prayer was just perfect for me as well. Thank you for allowing God to use you to minister and speak His Word to me. It is a blessing to my spirit. – Socratif

Spiritual Prayers
There are so many golden nuggets in your devotional this morning, Brother Boyd, but oh the one, "Taste His Grace," just fills my soul! God bless you. – Jenny

Sword of the Spirit
Thank you, Mr. Bailey, for Wisdom Hunters. I read it on my e-mail as much as I can. It is so uplifting, and I love that you list other Scriptures to follow up with that day's online message. God bless you in your work. – Carol

Window of Opportunity
I liked the devotional today about making use of windows of opportunities that God has given to me. Thank you for this post and the other daily posts, which reaffirm my faith and make me make right choices as I obey His Word. May God bless you and your family and all believers who are a part of this ministry. God bless you all. – Jonathan

I am very grateful to have this resource. These devotionals provide biblical truth appropriate to current situations. They help me hunger for more of God's Word in my daily walk. Thank you for being such an encouraging reminder that God really cares, wants the best for us, and has our backs, and all we have to do is walk in faithful obedience. – Noemi

BECOMING A DISCIPLE OF JESUS CHRIST

My process for finding God covered a span of 19 years, before I truly understood my need for His love and forgiveness in a personal relationship with Jesus Christ. Along this path of spiritual awakening people in my life contributed to my progress in knowing God.

My mother took me to church at age 12, so I could learn about faith through the confirmation process. My grandmother modeled her walk with Jesus by being kind and generous to all she encountered. In college I begin attending church with Rita (my future wife) and her family.

Weekly relevant teaching from an ancient book—the Bible—began to answer many of life's questions. It intrigued me: What is God's plan for my life? Who is Jesus Christ? What are sin, salvation, heaven and hell? How can I live an abundant life of forgiveness, joy and love?

So, the Lord found me first with His incredible love and when I surrendered in repentance and faith in Jesus, I found Him. For two years a businessman in our church showed me how to grow in grace through Bible study, prayer, faith sharing and service to others. I still discover each day more of God's great love and His new mercies.

Below is an outline for finding God and becoming a disciple of Jesus:

1. **BELIEVE:** "If you declare with your mouth, "Jesus is Lord," and believe in your heart that God raised him from the dead, you will be saved" (Romans 10:9). Belief in Jesus Christ as your Savior and Lord gives you eternal life in heaven.

2. **REPENT AND BE BAPTIZED:** "Peter replied, "Repent and be baptized, every one of you, in the name of Jesus Christ for the forgiveness of your sins. And you will receive the gift of the Holy Spirit" (Acts 2:38). Repentance means you turn from your sin and publically confess Christ in baptism.

3. OBEY: "Jesus replied, "Anyone who loves me will obey my teaching. My Father will love them, and we will come to them and make our home with them" (John 14:23).

4. WORSHIP, PRAYER, COMMUNITY, EVANGELISM AND STUDY: "Every day they continued to meet together in the temple courts. They broke bread in their homes and ate together with glad and sincere hearts, praising God and enjoying the favor of all the people. And the Lord added to their number daily those who were being saved" (Acts 2:46-47).

5. LOVE GOD: "Jesus replied: "'Love the Lord your God with all your heart and with all your soul and with all your mind.' This is the first and greatest commandment" (Matthew 22:37-38).

6. LOVE PEOPLE: "And the second is like it: 'Love your neighbor as yourself" (Matthew 22:39).

7. MAKE DISCIPLES: "And the things you have heard me say in the presence of many witnesses entrust to reliable people who will also be qualified to teach others" (2 Timothy 2:2).

MEET THE AUTHOR

Boyd Bailey

Boyd Bailey, the author of Wisdom Hunters devotionals, is the founder of Wisdom Hunters, Inc., an Atlanta-based ministry created to encourage Christians (a.k.a wisdom hunters) to *apply God's unchanging Truth in a changing world.*

By God's grace, Boyd has impacted wisdom hunters in over 86 countries across the globe through the Wisdom Hunters daily devotion, wisdomhunters.com devotional blog and devotional books.

For over 30 years Boyd Bailey has passionately pursued wisdom through his career in fulltime ministry, executive coaching, and mentoring.

Since becoming a Christian at the age of 19, Boyd begins each day as a wisdom hunter, diligently searching for Truth in scripture, and through God's grace, applying it to his life.

These raw, 'real time' reflections from his personal time with the Lord, are now impacting over 111,000 people through the Wisdom Hunters Daily Devotion email. In addition to the daily devotion, Boyd has authored nine devotional books: *Infusion*, a 90-day devotional, *Seeking Daily the Heart of God Vol I & II*, 365-day devotionals *Seeking God in the Proverbs*, a 90-day devotional and *Seeking God in the Psalms*, a 90-day devotional along with several 30-day devotional e-Books on topics such as *Wisdom for Fathers, Wisdom for Mothers, Wisdom for Graduates,* and *Wisdom for Marriage.*

In addition to Wisdom Hunters, Boyd is the co-founder and CEO of Ministry Ventures, a faith based non-profit, where he has trained and coached over 1000 ministries in the best practices of prayer, board, ministry models, administration and fundraising. Prior to Ministry Ventures, Boyd was the National Director for Crown Financial Ministries and an Associate Pastor at First Baptist Church of Atlanta. Boyd serves on numerous boards including Ministry Ventures, Wisdom Hunters, Atlanta Mission, Souly Business and Blue Print for Life.

Boyd received his Bachelor of Arts from Jacksonville State University and his Masters of Divinity from Southwestern Seminary. He and Rita, his wife of 30 plus years, live in Roswell, Georgia and are blessed with four daughters, three sons-in-law who love Jesus, two granddaughters and two grandsons. Boyd and Rita enjoy missions and investing in young couples, as well as hiking, reading, traveling, working through their bucket list, watching college football, and hanging out with their kids and grand kids when ever possible.